Houghton Mifflin

Math Expressions

Grade 1

Homework and Remembering

Developed by
**The Children's Math Worlds
Research Project**

PROJECT DIRECTOR AND AUTHOR
Dr. Karen C. Fuson

This material is based upon work supported by the
National Science Foundation
under Grant Numbers
ESI-9816320, REC-9806020, and

Any opinions, findings, and conclusions or recomm
material are those of the author and do not necess
National Science Foundatic

HOUGHTON MIFFLIN   BOSTON

Teacher Reviewers

Kindergarten

Patti Sugiyama
Wilmette, Illinois

Barbara Wahle
Evanston, Illinois

Grade 1

Megan Rees
Chicago, Illinois

Sandra Budson
Newton, Massachusetts

Grade 2

Janet Pecci
Chicago, Illinois

Molly Dunn
Danvers, Massachusetts

Agnes Lesnick
Hillside, Illinois

Grade 3

Sandra Tucker
Chicago, Illinois

Jane Curran
Honesdale, Pennsylvania

Grade 4

Sheri Roedel
Chicago, Illinois

Grade 5

Todd Atler
Chicago, Illinois

Leah Barry
Norfolk, Massachusetts

Credits

Cover art: (koala) © Royalty-Free/Corbis. (zebra) © Masahiro Iijima/Ardea London Ltd. (eucalyptus) © Victoria Pearson/Stone/Getty Images. (blocks) © HMCo./Richard Hutchings.

Illustrative art: Ginna Magee and Burgandy Beam/Wilkinson Studio; Tim Johnson
Technical art: Anthology, Inc.

Printed in the U.S.A.

ISBN: 0-618-64110-6

1 2 3 4 5 6 7 8 9 EB 11 10 09 08 07 06

Homework

1. Compare the cherry pies and the apples pies.
   Complete the sentences below.
   Ring the word **more** or **fewer**.

Apple								

There are ⬜ **more fewer** apple pies than cherry pies.

There are ⬜ **more fewer** cherry pies than apple pies.

---

2. Each bird gets 1 house.
   How many extra houses are there? ⬜

3. Cross out the extra houses.

Houses							
Birds							

---

4. Each dog gets 1 ball.
   How many more balls are needed? ⬜

5. Draw them on the graph.

Dogs									
Balls									

Name _____

Targeted Practice

Fill in the missing numbers.

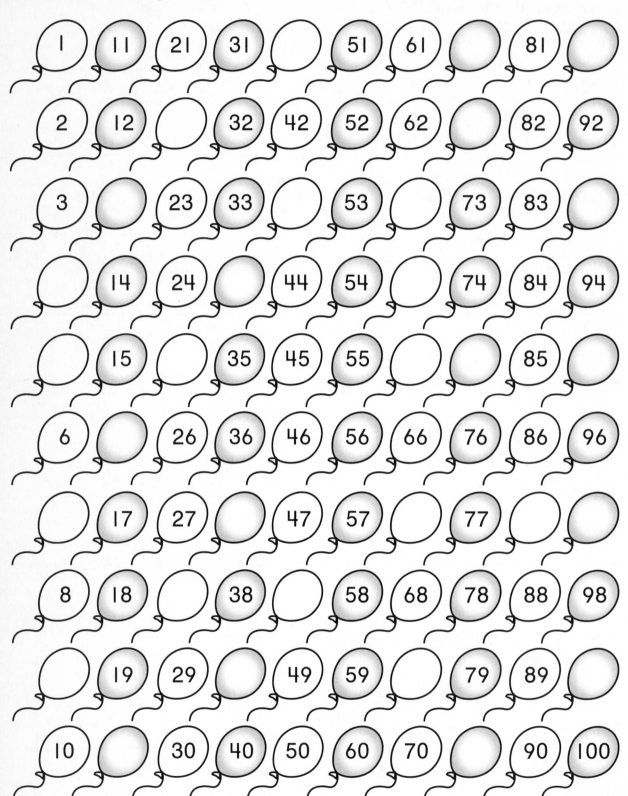

1	11	21	31		51	61		81	
2	12		32	42	52	62		82	92
3		23	33		53		73	83	
	14	24		44	54		74	84	94
	15		35	45	55			85	
6		26	36	46	56	66	76	86	96
	17	27		47	57		77		
8	18		38		58	68	78	88	98
	19	29		49	59		79	89	
10		30	40	50	60	70		90	100

Simple Comparisons and Graphs

Name _____

Homework

1. Make a picture graph about the balloons.

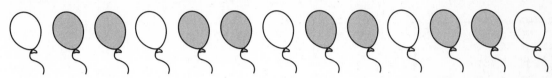

Gray Balloons							
White Balloons							

2. Complete the sentences. Ring the word **more** or **fewer**.

There are ☐ **more** **fewer** white balloons than gray balloons.

There are ☐ **more** **fewer** gray balloons than white balloons.

3. Make a picture graph about the people.

People with Hats							
People without Hats							

4. Complete the sentences. Ring the word **more** or **fewer**.

There are ☐ **more** **fewer** people with hats.

There are ☐ **more** **fewer** people without hats.

Construct Picture Graphs **155**

Targeted Practice

Draw a line to show the 100-partners. Fill in the answer box.

1.

$$100 = 60 + \boxed{}$$

2.

$$100 = 20 + \boxed{}$$

3.

$$100 = 30 + \boxed{}$$

4.

$$100 = 90 + \boxed{}$$

Solve the story problems.

5. Justin has 70 cents. How many more cents does he need to have a dollar?

 ¢

6. Ana had a dollar. She spent 50 cents. How many cents does she have now?

 ¢

Construct Picture Graphs

Homework

1. Kate ran 5 blocks. Ann ran 9 blocks.

   Draw dots on the graph to show how many blocks they ran.

Kate								
Ann								

2. Complete the sentences. Ring the word **more** or **fewer**.

   Kate ran ☐ **more fewer** blocks than Ann.

   Ann ran ☐ **more fewer** blocks than Kate.

   They ran ☐ blocks in all.

---

3. Dan did 4 jumps. Joel did 7 jumps.

   Draw dots on the graph to show how many jumps they did.

Dan							
Joel							

4. Complete the sentences. Ring the word **more** or **fewer**.

   Dan did ☐ **more fewer** jumps than Joel.

   Joel did ☐ **more fewer** jumps than Dan.

   They did ☐ jumps in all.

Remembering

1. Compare Yolanda's shells with Andrew's.
Complete the sentences below.
Ring the word **more** or **fewer**.

Yolanda									
Andrew									

Yolanda has ☐ **more fewer** shells than Andrew.

Andrew has ☐ **more fewer** shells than Yolanda.

Solve the equations.

2. 5 + 10 = ☐   **3.** 45 + 2 = ☐   **4.** 46 + 30 = ☐

5. 76 + 3 = ☐   **6.** 61 + 5 = ☐   **7.** 24 + 60 = ☐

8. 83 + 5 = ☐   **9.** 83 + 4 = ☐   **10.** 37 + 30 = ☐

Continue the numbers.

11. ⟨26⟩ ⟨36⟩ ⟨46⟩ ⟨ ⟩ ⟨ ⟩ ⟨ ⟩ ⟨ ⟩ ⟨ ⟩

12. ❁14 ❁24 ❁34 ❁ ❁ ❁ ❁ ❁

Quick Graphs and Comparisons

Homework

Buckets of Milk This Week

1. Which cow gave the fewest buckets of milk? _____

2. Which cow gave 8 buckets of milk? _____

3. How many more buckets of milk did Molly give than Greta? _____

Fish Caught at the Lake

Alonzo	🐟 🐟 🐟 🐟 🐟 🐟
Dana	🐟 🐟 🐟 🐟 🐟 🐟 🐟
Ramona	🐟 🐟 🐟 🐟

4. Who caught the most fish? _____

5. How many fewer fish did Ramona catch than Dana? _____

6. How many fish were caught altogether? _____

Targeted Practice

Pieces of Cheese Eaten This Week

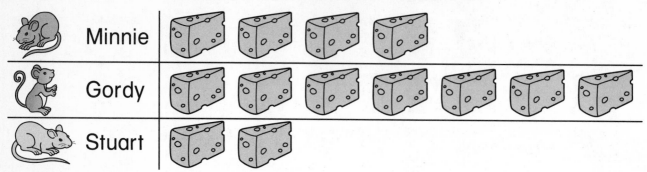

1. Which mouse ate the fewest pieces of cheese? _____

2. Which mouse ate 7 pieces of cheese? _____

3. How many more pieces of cheese did Gordy
eat than Stuart? _____

Pumpkins Sold at the Farm

4. On which day were the fewest pumpkins sold? _____

5. How many fewer pumpkins were sold on Sunday
than Saturday? _____

6. How many pumpkins were sold on Friday? _____

Graphs with Multiple Rows

Weather This Month

Sunny Days	☀ ☀ ☀ ☀ ☀ ☀ ☀ ☀ ☀
Cloudy Days	☁ ☁ ☁ ☁ ☁ ☁ ☁ ☁
Rainy Days	🌧 🌧 🌧 🌧 🌧

1. How many more sunny days were there than rainy days? _____

2. How many fewer rainy days were there than cloudy days? _____

3. How many cloudy days and rainy days were there in all? _____

Telephone Calls This Week

Nadia	📱 📱 📱 📱 📱 📱
Julio	📱 📱 📱 📱 📱 📱 📱 📱 📱
Adam	📱 📱 📱 📱 📱 📱

4. Who made the fewest telephone calls? _____

5. Who made 7 telephone calls? _____

6. How many more calls did Adam make than Nadia? _____

Remembering

1. Make a picture graph about the hearts.

White Hearts								
Gray Hearts								

2. Complete the sentences. Ring the word **more** or **fewer**.

There are [　　] **more** **fewer** white hearts than gray hearts.

There are [　　] **more** **fewer** gray hearts than white hearts.

3. Draw enough dimes and pennies to pay for the card.

4. Write the missing numbers.

14				18				

Homework

1. Use the empty picture graph. Show the number of letters in the first name of four people you know.

Number of Letters in Our Names

Leon	○	○	○	○				
Maria	○	○	○	○	○			
Ricardo	○	○	○	○	○	○	○	
Emilia	○	○	○	○	○	○		

Number of Letters in Our Names

Answer the questions about your graph.

2. Whose name has the most letters? _____

   How many letters? _____

3. Whose name has the fewest letters? _____

   How many letters? _____

Targeted Practice

Use the graphs to answer the questions.

Pet Birds

Jill	🐦 🐦 🐦 🐦 🐦 🐦 🐦
Mika	🐦 🐦 🐦 🐦 🐦
Leon	🐦 🐦 🐦

1. Who owns the most birds? _____

2. Who owns 5 birds? _____

3. How many more birds does Jill own than Leon? _____

Phone Calls Made at Tanya's House

Mom	📞 📞 📞
Dad	📞 📞 📞 📞 📞 📞
Tanya	📞 📞 📞 📞 📞 📞 📞 📞 📞

4. Who made the fewest calls? _____

5. How many more calls did Tanya make than Dad? _____

6. How many fewer calls did Mom make than Tanya? _____

Name _____

Homework

1. Make a table from the picture graph. Answer the questions.

Picture Graph

Ducks	🦆 🦆 🦆 🦆 🦆
Balls	⚽ ⚽ ⚽ ⚽
Kites	🪁 🪁 🪁 🪁 🪁 🪁

Table

Toys	Number

2. There is the fewest of which toy? _____

3. How many more kites are there than balls? _____

Answer the questions about the table below.

Beach Toys

Toys	Number
Buckets	12
Shovels	14
Beach Balls	7

4. How many more shovels are there than beach balls?

_____

5. How many fewer beach balls are there than buckets?

_____

6. There are the fewest of which beach toy?

_____

Remembering

Answer the questions about the picture graph.

Food at the Party

Sandwiches	🍔 🍔 🍔 🍔 🍔 🍔 🍔 🍔
Pizza Slices	🍕 🍕 🍕 🍕 🍕 🍕
Muffins	🧁 🧁 🧁 🧁 🧁

1. There are the most of which food? _____

2. There are the fewest of which food? _____

3. There are _____ more sandwiches than muffins.

4. There are _____ fewer pizza slices than sandwiches.

Complete the exercises.

5. $7 + 10 =$ ☐   **6.** $35 + 8 =$ ☐   **7.** $63 + 20 =$ ☐

8. $56 + 2 =$ ☐   **9.** $77 + 4 =$ ☐   **10.** $34 + 60 =$ ☐

11. $73 + 7 =$ ☐   **12.** $84 + 9 =$ ☐   **13.** $29 + 30 =$ ☐

From Picture Graphs to Tables

Name _____

Homework

Solve the story problems.

1. Janeka drew 4 houses.
Kelly drew 3 more
than Janeka.
How many houses
did Kelly draw?

[   ] _____
                label

2. Oak School has 9 computers.
Hill School has 4 computers.
How many fewer computers
does Hill School have?

[   ] _____
                label

3. Tony made 8 pots.
Lisa made 2 fewer
pots than Tony.
How many pots did
Lisa make?

[   ] _____
                label

Story Problems with Comparisons **167**

Targeted Practice

Make a table from the picture graph.
Answer the questions.

Food in the Kitchen

Fruit	🍓 🍓 🍓 🍓 🍓
Eggs	○ ○ ○ ○ ○ ○ ○
Bread	🍞 🍞 🍞 🍞

Table

Food	How Many

1. There is the most of which kind of food? _____

2. How many more eggs are there than loaves of bread?

_____

Answer the questions about the table below.

Things at the Park

Thing	Number
Swings	14
Slides	5
Sandboxes	7

3. How many more swings are there than sandboxes?

_____

4. How many fewer slides are there than swings?

_____

5. How many fewer slides are there than sandboxes?

_____

Story Problems with Comparisons

Homework

Solve the story problems.	**Show your work. Use pictures, numbers, or words.**

1. Toby has 12 balloons.
Roberto has 5 balloons.
How many more balloons does
Toby have than Roberto?

balloon

☐ _____
      label

2. Nora has 4 candles on her
cake. Maria has 9 more
candles than Nora. How many
candles does Maria have?

cake

☐ _____
      label

3. Meg bought 15 flags.
Alan has 6 fewer flags than
Meg. How many flags does
Alan have?

flag

☐ _____
      label

       Comparison Story Problem Strategies **169**

Name _____

Targeted Practice

Make a table from a graph.
Answer the questions.

Insects in the Garden

Bees	🐝 🐝 🐝 🐝 🐝
Ants	🐜 🐜 🐜 🐜 🐜 🐜 🐜 🐜
Crickets	🦗 🦗 🦗 🦗

Insects in the Garden

Insects	How Many

1. There are the fewest of which kind of insect? _____

2. How many more ants are there than bees? _____

Answer the questions about the table below.

Rides at the Fair

Rides	Number
Roller Coasters	7
Carousels	4
Trains	12

3. How many more trains are there than carousels?

_____

4. How many fewer carousels are there than roller coasters?

_____

5. There are the fewest of which kind of ride?

_____

Comparison Story Problem Strategies

Homework

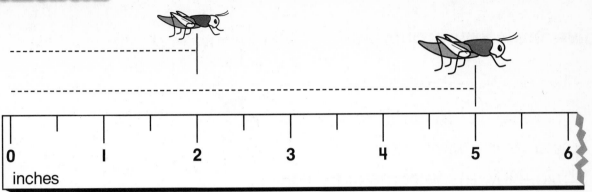

1. How far did the little cricket jump? _____ inches

2. How far did the big cricket jump? _____ inches

3. How much farther did the big cricket jump? _____ inches

Solve the story problems.	**Show your work. Use pictures, numbers, or words.**
4. Ramzan's shoe is 6 inches long. His father's shoe is 5 inches longer. How long is his father's shoe? ☐ _____ label	 shoe
5. Melissa caught a fish 12 inches long. Her sister caught a fish that was 4 inches shorter. How long was her sister's fish? ☐ _____ label	 fish

Remembering

Solve the story problems.

Show your work. Use pictures, numbers, or words.

1. Sonia saw 13 barns. Pedro saw 5 fewer barns than Sonia. How many barns did Pedro see?

barn

```
┌──────┐
│      │   _____
└──────┘
        label
```

Write how many circles.

2.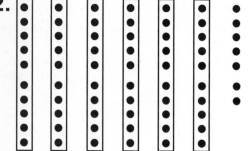

How many? ☐

3.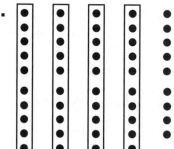

How many? ☐

Write the missing numbers.

4.

35 ☐ ☐ ☐ 39 ☐ ☐ ☐ ☐ ☐

Measurement with Inches

Name _____

Measure the chains. Complete the table.

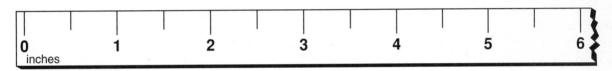
Paco's Chain

Leah's Chain

Tara's Chain

Reed's Chain

Chain	Length
Paco's Chain	
Leah's Chain	
Tara's Chain	
Reed's Chain	

1. How much shorter is Paco's chain
than Leah's chain?   _____

2. How much longer is Reed's chain
than Tara's chain?   _____

3. How much longer is Leah's chain than
Tara's chain?   _____

Name _____

Targeted Practice

Solve the story problems.	Show your work. Use pictures, numbers, or words.

1. 14 ducks are swimming in a pond. 8 ducks are walking on the shore. How many fewer ducks are walking than swimming?

duck

◻ _____
      label

2. Lynn's soccer team had 13 soccer balls. After the game, Lynn only found 9 balls. How many soccer balls did the team lose?

soccer ball

◻ _____
      label

3. Kim jumped 16 times with her jump rope. Evan jumped 8 times with his jump rope. How many more times did Kim jump than Evan?

jump rope

◻ _____
      label

Measurement Tables

Homework

Draw the next shape in each row.

1.

2.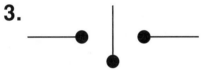

3.

4.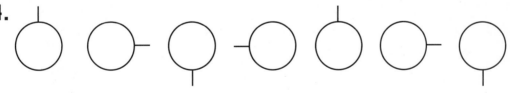

5.

Name _____

Targeted Practice

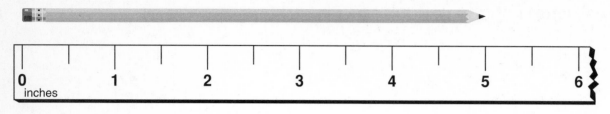

1. How long is the big pencil? _____ inches

2. How long is the small pencil? _____ inches

3. How much longer is the big pencil? _____ inches

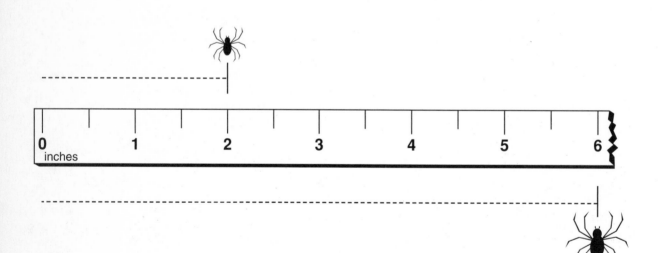

1. How far did the small spider crawl? _____ inches

2. How far did the big spider crawl? _____ inches

3. How much farther did the big spider crawl? _____ inches

Comparison and Rotation of Shapes

Name _____

Homework

Make each shape on the triangle grid.

1. Make a
   parallelogram.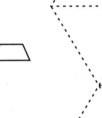
   Color it red.

2. Make a trapezoid.
   Color it blue.

3. Make a hexagon.
   Color it green.

Draw the next shape in each row below.

4.
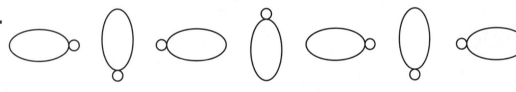

5.
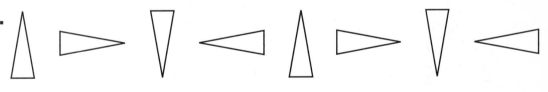

6.

Name _____

Remembering

Measure and compare the bookmarks.

1. Raul's bookmark   How long? _____ inches

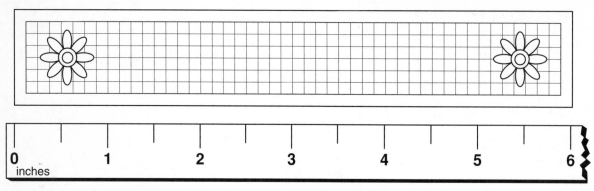

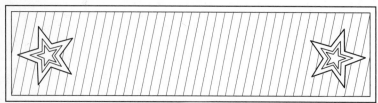

2. John's bookmark   How long? _____ inches

3. How much longer is Raul's bookmark than John's?

_____ inches

Draw enough dimes and pennies to pay for the basket.

4.

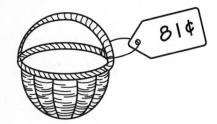

81¢

Shape Combinations

Name

Homework

1. Color the trapezoids ⬜ blue.

Color the parallelograms ▱ red.

Color the hexagons ⬡ green.

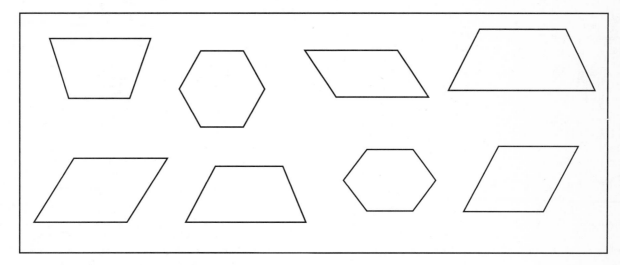

2. Color the cubes ⬜ yellow.

Color the cylinders ⬭ green.

Color the rectangular prisms ▭ blue.

Color the cones △ red.

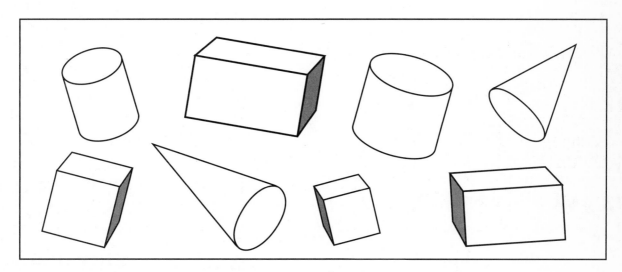

Exploration of Solid Shapes **179**

Name _____

Remembering

Draw the next shape in each row.

1.

2.

Add the numbers.

3. 8 + 10 = ☐   **4.** 44 + 8 = ☐   **5.** 29 + 30 = ☐

6. 56 + 3 = ☐   **7.** 87 + 5 = ☐   **8.** 15 + 60 = ☐

9. 73 + 9 = ☐   **10.** 79 + 4 = ☐   **11.** 32 + 40 = ☐

Continue the pattern.

12. 25 35 45

13. 13 23 33

Exploration of Solid Shapes

Name _____

Homework

Ring the doubles.

Write an equation for each.

1. ⊙⊙ • $\underline{1} + \underline{1} = \underline{2}$

2. ⬭ ⬭ • $\underline{2} + \underline{2} = \underline{4}$

3. ⬭ ⬭ • • • • • • • • • • • • • • • • • • $\underline{3} + \underline{3} = \underline{6}$

4. •   ___ + ___ = ___

5. •   ___ + ___ = ___

6. •   ___ + ___ = ___

7. •   ___ + ___ = ___

8. •   ___ + ___ = ___

9. •   ___ + ___ = ___

10. •   ___ + ___ = ___

Make each rectangle twice as big.

11.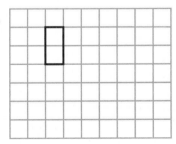

12.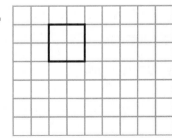

13.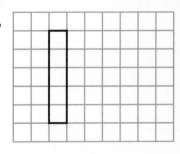

Targeted Practice

Solve the story problems.	**Show your work. Use pictures, numbers, or words.**

1. Gina has 5 balloons.

Tasha has 7 more balloons than Gina.

How many balloons does Tasha have?

☐ _____
        label

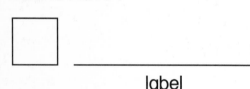
balloon

---

2. Leah played the piano for 15 minutes.

Julio played the piano for 9 minutes.

How many fewer minutes did Julio play?

☐ _____
        label

piano

---

3. The white cat had 12 kittens.

The grey cat had 8 kittens.

How many fewer kittens did the grey cat have than the white cat?

☐ _____
        label

kitten

Homework

Solve the story problems.	**Show your work. Use pictures, numbers, or words.**
1. There are 9 seals on the rocks. There are twice as many in the water. How many seals are in the water? ☐ _____ label	seal
2. We saw 7 ants on the picnic table. Then the number of ants doubled. How many ants are there now? ☐ _____ label	picnic table

Add the numbers.

3. 6 + 6 = ☐

4. 8 + 8 = ☐

5. 8 + 9 = ☐

6. 9 + 9 = ☐

7. 5 + 5 = ☐

8. 7 + 8 = ☐

9. 7 + 7 = ☐

10. 10 + 10 = ☐

11. 6 + 7 = ☐

Name _____

Remembering

Solve the story problem.	**Show your work. Use pictures, numbers, or words.**
1. I have 8 fish. My sister has twice as many fish. How many fish does my sister have? [ ] _____ label	fish

Answer the questions about the picture graph.

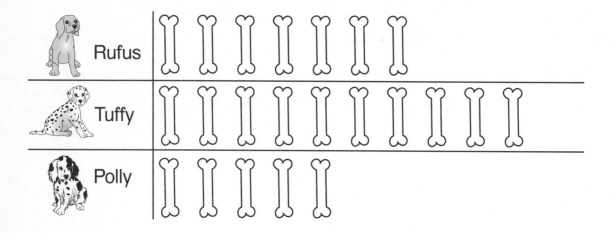

2. How many more bones does Tuffy have than Rufus? _____

3. How many fewer bones does Polly have than Tuffy? _____

4. How many more bones does Rufus have than Polly? _____

5. Which dog has twice as many bones as Polly? _____

Problem Solve with Doubles

Homework

Count the objects. Ring half of them.
Then fill in the blanks.

 Half of __6__ is __3__.

1.  Half of ____ is ____.

2. Half of ____ is ____.

3.  Half of ____ is ____.

Solve the story problems.	**Show your work. Use pictures, numbers, or words.**
4. There were 12 pennies in my pocket yesterday. Now there are only half as many. How many pennies are there now? [ ] _____ label	 pocket
5. There are 16 animals at the pet show. Half of them are dogs. How many dogs are there? [ ] _____ label	dog

Targeted Practice

Solve the story problems.

	Show your work. Use pictures, numbers, or words.

I. Leon has 9 shells.

Regina has 8 more shells than Leon.

How many shells does Regina have?

shell

☐ _____
label

2. There are 14 blue flowers in the garden.

There are 6 yellow flowers.

How many more blue flowers are there than yellow flowers?

flower

☐ _____
label

3. Justin traded 13 marbles.

Maria traded 4 fewer marbles than Justin.

How many marbles did Maria trade?

marble

☐ _____
label

The Meaning of Half

Homework

Draw one line of symmetry for each shape below.

1.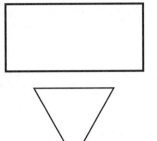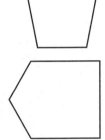

Ring half of the objects in each group.
Then fill in the blanks.

2. Half of ____ is ____.

3. Half of ____ is ____.

4. Half of ____ is ____.

Solve the story problem. **Label the answer.**	**Show your work. Use pictures, numbers, or words.**
5. Raul has 9 cents. Anna has twice as much. How many cents does Anna have? ☐ _____ label	 cent

Remembering

Count the animals.
Ring one half.
Then fill in the blanks.

1. 🐪🐪🐪🐪🐪🐪🐪🐪   Half of ____ is ____.

2. 🦩🦩🦩🦩🦩🦩🦩🦩🦩🦩   Half of ____ is ____.

3. 🦒🦒🦒🦒🦒🦒🦒🦒🦒🦒   Half of ____ is ____.

4. 🦌🦌🦌🦌🦌🦌   Half of ____ is ____.

**Solve the story problem.
Label the answer.**

| **Show your work. Use pictures, numbers, or words.**

5. My brother has 15 marbles.

    I have 7 fewer marbles than he does.

    How many marbles do I have?

marble

⬜ _____
       label

Complete the exercises.

6. $9 + 8 =$ ⬜   **7.** $15 - 8 =$ ⬜   **8.** $8 +$ ⬜ $= 12$

9. $6 + 7 =$ ⬜   **10.** $14 - 5 =$ ⬜   **11.** $7 +$ ⬜ $= 16$

Name _____

Homework

Ring one fourth of the objects. Then fill in the blanks.

 One fourth of __4__ is __1__.

1.  One fourth of ____ is ____.

2.  One fourth of ____ is ____.

3. 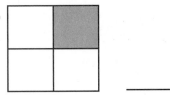 One fourth of ____ is ____.

How much is shaded? Write $\frac{1}{2}$ or $\frac{1}{4}$ on each line.

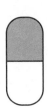 $\frac{1}{2}$

4.  ____

5. ____

6. ____

7. 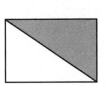 ____

8. 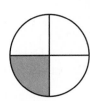 ____

9.  ____

10.  ____

11.  ____

Fraction Notation and Fourths **189**

Targeted Practice

What part of each shape is shaded? Write $\frac{1}{2}$ or $\frac{1}{4}$ in each box.

 $\frac{1}{4}$

1. ☐ **2.** ☐

3. 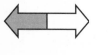 ☐ **4.** ☐ **5.** 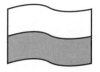 ☐

6. ☐ **7.** ☐ **8.**  ☐

9. ☐ **10.** 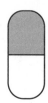 ☐ **11.** ☐

12. ☐ **13.** ☐ **14.** 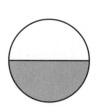 ☐

15. ☐ **16.** ☐ **17.** ☐

18. Choose Ring the shape that best shows how two fourths equal one half.

Fraction Notation and Fourths

Homework

Write how many cents.

1.   ¢

2.   ¢

3.   ¢

Solve the story problems.

4. Mrs. Chan has a dollar.

   She wants to give equal shares to her 4 children.

   How many cents should she give each child?   ¢

5. Cesar had 50 cents.

   Then he spent a quarter.

   How many cents does he have left?   ¢

6. Ali has 3 quarters.

   How many cents does he have?   ¢

Name _____

Remembering

How much is shaded? Write $\frac{1}{2}$ or $\frac{1}{4}$ in each box.

1. ⬜

2. ⬜

3. 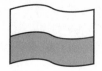 ⬜

4. ⬜

5.  ⬜

6. ⬜

Solve the story problem.
Label the answer.

Show your work. Use pictures, numbers, or words.

7. Isabel has 12 crayons.

Jay has 6 fewer than Isabel.

How many crayons does Jay have?

⬜ _____
label

crayon

Add the numbers.

8. 57
  + 40

9. 32
  + 30

10. 29
  + 60

11. 18
  + 70

12. 46
  + 50

Halves and Fourths of a Dollar

Homework

What part of each shape is shaded?

1. 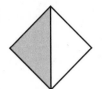 $\frac{1}{4}$	**2.** 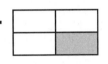	**3.** 
4. 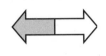	**5.**	**6.** 
7.	**8.**	**9.**

What part of each group of apples was eaten?

10.

11.

Complete the exercises.

12. Half of 8 is _____.

13. One fourth of 12 is _____.

14. Half of 10 is _____.

15. One fourth of a dollar is _____ ¢.

16. Half a dollar is _____ ¢.

17. Shade one fourth of this circle.

Name _____

Targeted Practice

Solve the story problems.	Show your work. Use pictures, numbers, or words.

1. There are 9 seals on the shore.

There are twice as many in the ocean.

How many seals are in the ocean?

seal

[ ] _____
label

---

2. We saw 7 ants by the tree.

Then the number of ants doubled.

How many ants are there now?

ant

[ ] _____
label

---

3. Add the numbers.

6 + 6 = [ ]   8 + 8 = [ ]   8 + 9 = [ ]

9 + 9 = [ ]   5 + 5 = [ ]   7 + 8 = [ ]

7 + 7 = [ ]   10 + 10 = [ ]   6 + 7 = [ ]

Practice with Halves and Fourths

Homework

Fill in the blanks.

Toys in the Playroom

1. One half of the toys are

_____ .

2. What fraction of the toys

are puzzles? _____

3. The total number of toys

is _____ .

4. There are twice as many

_____ as dolls.

5. Finish the circle graph.

Amanda had a dollar.
Here is how she spent it.

25¢ on a toy

25¢ on gum

25¢ on a pen

25¢ on a bow

Amanda's Dollar

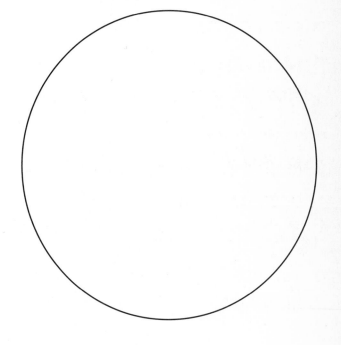

Introduction to Circle Graphs and Probability **195**

Name _____

Targeted Practice

Write how many cents.

1.

 ¢

2.

 ¢

3.

 ¢

Solve the story problems.

4. Miranda had a dollar. Then she spent a quarter. How many cents does she have now?

 ¢

5. Hunter has 25 cents. How many more cents does he need to have a dollar?

 ¢

6. Tim has 2 quarters. How many cents does he have?

 ¢

Introduction to Circle Graphs and Probability

Homework

Make a table from the circle graph. Then answer the questions.

School Supplies

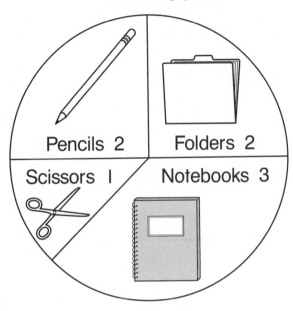

Pencils 2   Folders 2

Scissors 1   Notebooks 3

Table

Kind of Supplies	Number

1. Which are there the most of? _____

2. Which are there the fewest of? _____

3. How many more notebooks are there than scissors? _____

4. How many fewer pencils are there than notebooks? _____

5. How many school supplies are there altogether? _____

6. The folders are what fraction of the total? _____

Name _____

Targeted Practice

Animals at the Zoo

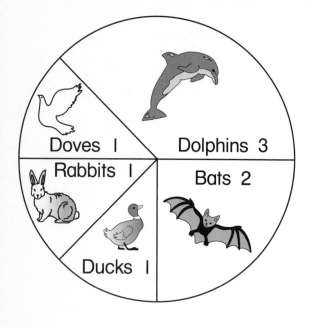

Doves 1

Dolphins 3

Rabbits 1

Bats 2

Ducks 1

1. The zoo has the most of which animal? _____

2. How many more bats are there than ducks? _____

3. How many fewer doves are there than dolphins? _____

4. There are the same number

   of _____,

   _____, and

   _____.

Animals on the Farm

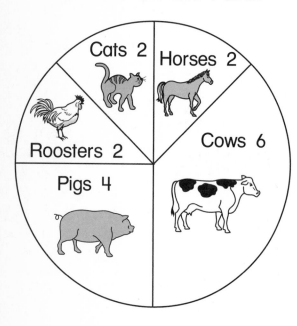

Cats 2

Horses 2

Roosters 2

Cows 6

Pigs 4

5. How many more cows are there than horses? _____

6. How many fewer roosters are there than pigs? _____

7. The farm has the most of which animal? _____

8. How many animals are there altogether? _____

Comparisons with Circle Graphs

Name

Homework

Write the time in the boxes.

1.

:

2.

:

3.

:

4.

:

5.

:

6.

:

Draw the time on the clocks.

7.

10:00

8.

2:00

9.

7:00

Clocks and Units of Time **199**

Remembering

Solve the story problem.

Show your work. Use pictures, numbers, or words.

1. I had 50 cents.

Then I spent a quarter.

How many cents do I have now?

quarter

⬜ ¢

Answer the questions about the picture graph.

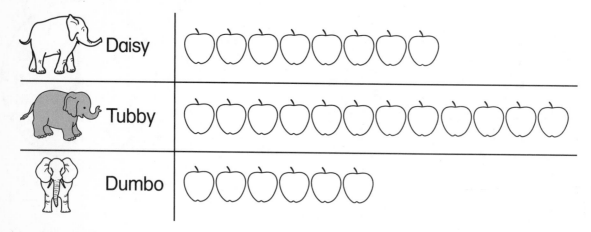

2. How many more apples did Tubby eat than Daisy? _____

3. How many fewer apples did Dumbo eat than Daisy? _____

4. How many apples did the elephants eat altogether? _____

5. Which elephant ate half as many apples as Tubby?

_____

Clocks and Units of Time

Homework

| Dog | Cat | Mouse | Bird | Hamster | Fish | Lizard | Turtle |

Write the animal in each position.

1. first _____

2. second _____

3. third _____

4. fourth _____

5. fifth _____

6. sixth _____

7. seventh _____

8. eighth _____

9. last _____

Name the position of the animal.

10. bird _____

11. cat _____

12. fish _____

13. dog _____

14. turtle _____

15. hamster _____

16. lizard _____

17. mouse _____

18. Color the first circle green, the second circle blue, and the third circle red.

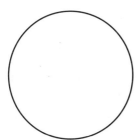 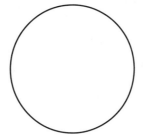 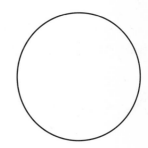

Targeted Practice

Write the time in the boxes.

1.

[:]

2.

[:]

3.

[:]

4.

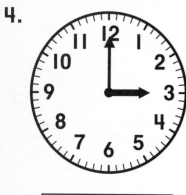

[:]

5.

[:]

6.

[:]

Draw the time on the clocks.

7.

8:00

8.

10:00

9.

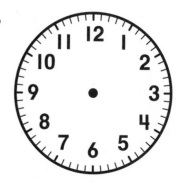

2:00

　　　　　　　Time and Ordinal Numbers

Homework

Write the time in the boxes.

1.

[:]

2.

[:]

3.

[:]

4.

[:]

5.

[:]

6.

[:]

Draw the time on the clocks.

7.

[9:30]

8.

[3:00]

9.

[8:30]

Targeted Practice

Write the time in the boxes.

1.

:

2.

:

3.

:

4.

:

5.

:

6.

:

Draw the time on the clocks.

7.

9:30

8.

1:00

9.
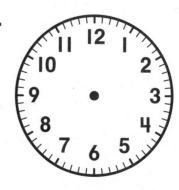

4:30

Tell Time to the Half-Hour

Homework

Name _____

Write the time.

1.

[:   ]

2.

[:   ]

3.

[:   ]

Draw the time on each clock.

4.

[11:30]

5.

[9:00]

6.

[2:30]

7.

[5:30]

Count the money.

8.

[   ] ¢

9.

[   ] ¢

10.

[   ] ¢

Remembering

Answer the questions about the circle graph.

Fruits in the Basket

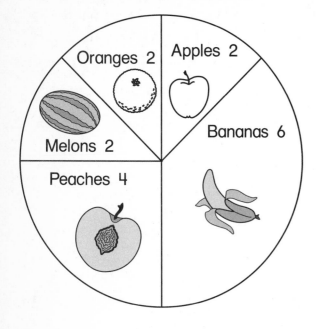

Oranges 2 Apples 2
Melons 2
Peaches 4
Bananas 6

1. How many more bananas are there than apples? _____

2. How many fewer melons are there than peaches? _____

3. The basket has the most of which fruit? _____

4. There are twice as many _____ as melons.

Write the number.

5. |||| ○○○○ ▢

6. |||| ○○○○○ ○ ▢

7. |||| || ○○ ▢

Draw sticks and circles.

8. 47

9. 71

10. 63

Consolidation: Clocks and Graphs

Name _____

Homework

Show the price with sticks and circles.
Write how many of each coin.

1.

Sticks and Circles

67¢   Dimes _____ Nickels _____ Pennies _____

2.

Sticks and Circles

49¢   Dimes _____ Nickels _____ Pennies _____

3.

Sticks and Circles

85¢   Dimes _____ Nickels _____ Pennies _____

4.

Sticks and Circles

56¢   Dimes _____ Nickels _____ Pennies _____

Targeted Practice

Make a table of the balls in the circle graph.

Then write the labels and circles on the picture graph below.

Balls at the Gym

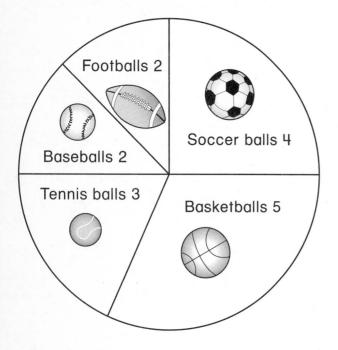

Footballs 2

Baseballs 2

Tennis balls 3

Soccer balls 4

Basketballs 5

Table

Kind of Balls	Number
Footballs	2
Soccer balls	
Basketballs	
Tennis balls	
Baseballs	

Picture Graph

Footballs	◯	◯			

Dimes, Nickels, and Pennies

Name _____

Homework

Solve the story problems.	Show your work. Use pictures, numbers, or words.
1. Emma has 8 dimes, 1 nickel, and 4 pennies in her purse. How many cents does she have? [ ]¢	 purse
2. Dan has 5 dimes, 1 nickel, and 2 pennies in his pocket. How many cents does he have? [ ]¢	pocket

How many cents?

3.   [ ]¢

 10   10   10   10   5   1   1

4.   [ ]¢

 10   10   10   5   1   1   1

5.    [ ]¢

___ ___ ___ ___ ___ ___

Targeted Practice

Write the time.

1.

```
[  :  ]
```

2.

```
[  :  ]
```

3.

```
[  :  ]
```

4.

```
[  :  ]
```

5.

```
[  :  ]
```

6.

```
[  :  ]
```

Draw the hands to show the time.

7.

```
3:30
```

8.

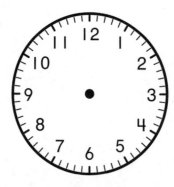

```
11:00
```

9.

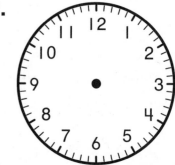

```
5:30
```

     Find Equivalent Coins and Values

Homework

Solve the story problems.	Show your work. Use pictures, numbers, or words.
1. Gwen bought a fish for 5 dimes, 1 nickel, and 7 pennies. How many cents did she spend? ☐ ¢	fish
2. Arturo has 7 dimes, 1 nickel, and 8 pennies in his pocket. How many cents does he have? ☐ ¢	pocket

What is the total price for each pair?

3. 57¢   8¢   ☐ ¢

4.  75¢    6¢   ☐ ¢

5.  68¢    9¢   ☐ ¢

Name _____

Remembering

Measure and compare the ribbons.

1. Julia's ribbon How long? _____ inches

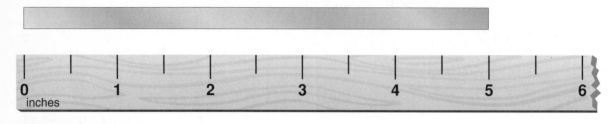
inches

2. Paulo's ribbon How long? _____ inches

3. How much longer is Julia's ribbon than Paulo's? _____ inches

---

4. Continue the numbers.

Draw the hands on the clocks to show the time.

5.

| 12:30 |

6.

| 7:00 |

7.

| 3:30 |

8.

| 2:00 |

Make Coin Conversions

Homework

1. How many apples? Write each number. How many apples
do Nick and Sarah have altogether? Write the total.

Nick's Apples

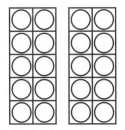

How many?

Sarah's Apples

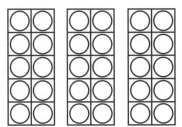

How many?

Total

Add the numbers with sticks and circles.

2.   37
      + 46

Total

---

3.   56
      + 28

Total

---

4.   29
      + 63

Total

Name _____

Targeted Practice

How many cents?

1.

   10   10   10   10   5   I   I   I

   [ ] ¢

2.

   [ ] ¢

   ___ ___ ___ ___ ___ ___ ___

3.

   [ ] ¢

   ___ ___ ___ ___ ___ ___ ___

Solve the story problems.

4.    Hannah has 7 dimes, I nickel, and 3 pennies. How many cents does she have?

   [ ] ¢

5.    Will paid 5 dimes, I nickel, and 4 pennies for a shell. How many cents did he pay?

   [ ] ¢

Explore Multi-Digit Addition

Homework

Solve with numbers, and with sticks and circles.

1. 37
   + 45
	2. 16
	   + 57

3. 25
   + 39
	4. 81
	   + 17

Solve the story problem.

Show your work. Use pictures, numbers, or words.

---

5. Yesterday, Kirsten counted
   29 butterflies. Today, she counted
   37 butterflies. How many butterflies
   did she count in all?

butterfly

◻️ _____
   label

Targeted Practice

1. How many apples? Write each number. How many apples do Tom and Bev have altogether? Write the total.

Tom's Apples

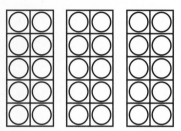  

How many? ☐

Bev's Apples

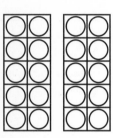  

How many? ☐

Total ☐

Solve with numbers, and with sticks and circles.

2. 28
     + 45

Total ☐

---

3. 54
     + 37

Total ☐

---

4. 69
     + 25

Total ☐

Student Methods: 2-Digit Addition

Homework

Add the numbers. Make a proof picture with sticks and circles.

1.　67 　　+ 26	**2.**　32 　　+ 37
3.　38 　　+ 47	**4.**　53 　　+ 39

5. How many nuts are there in all?

　　　　　　　　　Addition of Tens and Ones **217**

Name _____

Remembering

How much is shaded? Write $\frac{1}{2}$ or $\frac{1}{4}$ in each box.

1.  ☐

2. ☐

3. ☐

4. ☐

5.  ☐

6. ☐

Add the numbers.

7. 48
   + 20

8. 64
   + 30

9. 27
   + 50

10. 19
   + 70

Solve the story problem.	**Show your work. Use pictures, numbers, or words.**
11. Lucy had 9 pencils. Then she got 7 more pencils. How many pencils does she have in all? ☐ _____ label	 pencil

Continue the pattern.

| 5 | 10 | 15 | | | | | | | | | |

Addition of Tens and Ones

Add the numbers. Make a proof picture with sticks and circles.

1.   56
    + 28
	2. 77
	    + 21

3.   47
    + 25
	4. 34
	    + 49

5. How many hats are there in all?

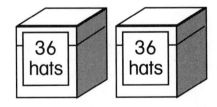

Targeted Practice

How many cents?

1.   ☐ ¢

    10   10   10   5   I   I   I   I

2.   ☐ ¢

   ___ ___ ___ ___ ___ ___ ___

3.   ☐ ¢

   ___ ___ ___ ___ ___ ___ ___

Solve the story problems.

Show your work. Use pictures, numbers, or words.

4. Ricardo bought a banana for 3 dimes, 1 nickel, and 2 pennies. How much did he pay?

   ☐ ¢

banana

5. Ruth has 9 dimes, 1 nickel, and 3 pennies in her pocket. How much money does she have?

   ☐ ¢

pocket

Name _____

Homework

Add the numbers. Then make a proof picture.

1.   28
   + 56
   ————
	2. 16
	   + 29
	   ————

How many peaches were picked by each pair?

3. Amy 26 Ali 33	4. Bert 18 Buffy 39
5. Carlos 16 Corky 39	6. Dora 49 Daniel 42

Remembering

Ring one half of the buildings. Then fill in the blanks.

1.   Half of ____ is ____.

2.   Half of ____ is ____.

3. 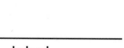   Half of ____ is ____.

Add the numbers.

4. 8 + 10 = ☐

5. 46 + 5 = ☐

6. 59 + 4 = ☐

7. 73 + 6 = ☐

Solve the story problem.	**Show your work. Use pictures, numbers, or words.**
8. I had 18 crayons. Then I lost 9 of them. How many crayons do I have now? ☐ _____ label	 crayon

---

How many cents?

9.   ☐ ¢

___ ___ ___ ___

Practice 2-Digit Addition

Name

Homework

Solve the story problems.	Show your work. Use pictures, numbers, or words.
1. There are 24 bikes behind the school and 19 bikes in front. What is the total number of bikes? ☐ _____ label	 bike
2. A quilt has 49 white pieces and 38 red pieces. How many pieces are there altogether? ☐ _____ label	 quilt

Add the numbers.

3. 68 + 28	**4.** 49 + 13	**5.** 72 + 26

Targeted Practice

Add the numbers. Did you make a new ten?

1. 56
    + 28

New ten?

yes ☐   no ☐

2. 29
    + 37

New ten?

yes ☐   no ☐

3. 42
    + 19

New ten?

yes ☐   no ☐

4. 74
    + 25

New ten?

yes ☐   no ☐

5. 47
    + 27

New ten?

yes ☐   no ☐

6. 13
    + 54

New ten?

yes ☐   no ☐

7. 65
    + 32

New ten?

yes ☐   no ☐

8. 69
    + 23

New ten?

yes ☐   no ☐

2-Digit Story Problems

Homework

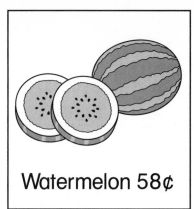

Watermelon 58¢

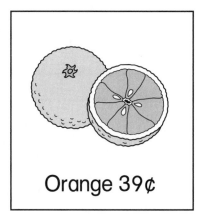

Orange 39¢

Bananas 47¢

Lemons 28¢

I. Cesar bought a watermelon and an orange. How much did he spend?

 ¢

How many dimes? _____

How many nickels? _____

How many pennies? _____

2. Carla bought bananas and lemons. How much did she spend?

 ¢

How many dimes? _____

How many nickels? _____

How many pennies? _____

Real-World Problems: 2-Digit Addition **225**

Name _____

Remembering

Ring one fourth. Then fill in the blanks.

1.   One fourth of ___ is ___.

2.   One fourth of ___ is ___.

3. ♡ ♡ ♡ ♡ ♡ ♡ ♡ ♡   One fourth of ___ is ___.

4. ☆☆☆☆☆☆☆☆☆☆☆☆☆☆☆☆   One fourth of ___ is ___.

Count the money in each row.

5. [quarter quarter quarter]   [ ] ¢

6. [quarter quarter quarter quarter]   [ ] ¢

Solve the story problem.	**Show your work. Use pictures, numbers, or words.**
7. We baked 8 muffins. Then we baked 6 more. How many muffins did we bake in all? [ ] _____ label	 muffin

Real-World Problems: 2-Digit Addition

Homework

Solve the problems with sticks and circles.

1. 64 + ☐ = 93

2. 18 + ☐ = 51

3. 49 + ☐ = 76

4. 27 + ☐ = 82

Solve the story problem.	**Show your work. Use pictures, numbers, or words.**
5. Raul has read 19 pages. He needs to read 32 in all. How many more pages does he need to read? ☐ _____ label	 page

Name

Remembering

How many cents?

1.

5   5   5   5   5   5   5

[   ] ¢

2.

___ ___ ___ ___ ___ ___ ___

[   ] ¢

Write the time below each clock.

3.

[:]

4.

[:]

5.

[:]

6.

[:]

Solve the story problem.

Show your work. Use pictures, numbers, or words.

7. There were 15 birds.

7 flew away.

How many birds are left?

[   ] _____

label

bird

2-Digit Addition: Unknown Partners

Homework

Solve the story problems.	Show your work. Use pictures, numbers, or words.

1. Paco has 62 cents. He wants to buy a toy sailboat for 1 dollar. How much more does he need?

☐ ¢

sailboat

2. Dana has 45 cents. She wants to buy some crayons that cost 1 dollar. How much more does she need?

☐ ¢

crayon

3. Carl wants to buy a notebook for 1 dollar. He has 37 cents. How much more does he need?

☐ ¢

notebook

4. Tess has 54 cents. She wants to buy some flowers that cost 1 dollar. How much more does she need?

☐ ¢

flower

Name _____

Targeted Practice

Solve the problems with sticks and circles.

1. 67 + ☐ = 90

2. 15 + ☐ = 62

3. 39 + ☐ = 75

4. 47 + ☐ = 100

Solve the story problem.	**Show your work. Use pictures, numbers, or words.**
5. Ana made a necklace with 16 beads. It needs to have 32. How many more beads should she put on the necklace?	necklace

☐ _____
        label

Unknown Partners of a Dollar

Name

Homework

Use sticks and circles to make change for a dollar.

1.

Yogurt 56¢

Change = [   ] ¢

2.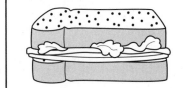

Sandwich 65¢

Change = [   ] ¢

3.

Milk 72¢

Change = [   ] ¢

4.

Muffin 48¢

Change = [   ] ¢

Name _____

Targeted Practice

Use sticks and circles to make change for a dollar.

1.

   Soup 49¢

   Change = [   ] ¢

2.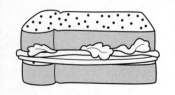

   Sandwich 68¢

   Change = [   ] ¢

3.

   Milk 76¢

   Change = [   ] ¢

4.

   Pickles 12¢

   Change = [   ] ¢

Make Change for a Dollar

Name _____

Homework

Solve the story problems.	**Show your work. Use pictures, numbers, or words.**
1. Ted has 12 cousins. 8 live on a farm. The others live in the city. How many cousins live in the city? ☐ _____ label	 city
2. Today 9 geese landed in our yard. Then 7 more geese came. How many geese are there in all? ☐ _____ label	 goose
3. Nicole had 13 buttons on her coat. Only 8 are left. How many buttons are lost? ☐ _____ label	 button
4. Nathan saw 16 windmills. Only 9 were working. How many were not working? ☐ _____ label	 windmill

Name _____

Targeted Practice

Add the numbers.

Did you make a new ten?

1.   42
   + 29
 	
               New ten?
           yes ☐   no ☐
	2. 25
	   + 38
	
	               New ten?
	           yes ☐ no ☐

3.   63
   + 24
 	
               New ten?
           yes ☐   no ☐
	4. 72
	   + 18
	
	               New ten?
	           yes ☐ no ☐

5.   58
   + 38
 	
               New ten?
           yes ☐   no ☐
	6. 17
	   + 74
	
	               New ten?
	           yes ☐ no ☐

7.   69
   + 26
 	
               New ten?
           yes ☐   no ☐
	8. 41
	   + 35
	
	               New ten?
	           yes ☐ no ☐

       Teen Problems with Various Unknowns

Name _____

Homework

Solve the story problems.

Show your work. Use pictures, numbers, or words.

---

1. My music book has 56 songs.
Your book has 32 songs.
How many songs do we have in all?

music book

☐ _____
label

---

2. Our vacation was 21 days long.
There were 13 days of rain.
How many days were not rainy?

rain

☐ _____
label

---

3. A pet store sold 48 fish yesterday
and 37 fish today. How many fish
were sold in all?

fish

☐ _____
label

---

4. There were 16 people on the ferris
wheel. Then some more people got
on. Now there are 34. How many
more people got on the ferris wheel?

ferris wheel

☐ _____
label

Name _____

Targeted Practice

Solve the story problems.

Show your work. Use pictures, numbers, or words.

---

1. Sam made 24 pots and Tyler made 38. How many pots did they make in all?

pot

[ ] _____
label

---

2. There were 17 bears playing. 9 played hide-and-seek. The others played tag. How many played tag?

bear

[ ] _____
label

---

3. Marty has 15 toy trucks. 8 are blue, and the rest of them are red. How many trucks are red?

truck

[ ] _____
label

---

4. At a magic show, 18 rabbits jumped out of a hat. Then 24 more jumped out. How many rabbits jumped out of the hat altogether?

rabbit

[ ] _____
label

Story Problems to 100

Name _____

Homework

Solve the story problems.	**Show your work. Use pictures, numbers, or words.**
1. I see 13 pieces of fruit on the table. 8 are oranges and the rest are lemons. How many are lemons? [ ] _____ label	 orange
2. There are 7 barns and 7 houses on River Road. How many buildings are there altogether? [ ] _____ label	 barn
3. At the pet show there are 15 animals. 6 are cats and the rest are dogs. How many are dogs? [ ] _____ label	 cat
4. There are 6 dolls and 7 teddy bears on the shelf. How many toys are there in all? [ ] _____ label	 teddy bear

Introduction to Category Problems **237**

Name _____

Remembering

How many cents?

1.   ¢

    10   10   10   10   5   1   1

2.   ¢

___ ___ ___ ___ ___ ___ ___ ___

Add the numbers.

3. 10 + 8 = ☐ | 4. 39 + 5 = ☐ | 5. 75 + 20 = ☐

6. 48 + 4 = ☐ | 7. 62 + 7 = ☐ | 8. 29 + 40 = ☐

9. Solve the story problem.

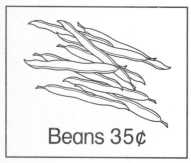

Beans 35¢

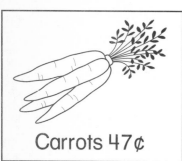

Carrots 47¢

Emilio bought beans and carrots.
How much did he spend?

☐ ¢

How many dimes? _____

How many nickels? _____

How many pennies? _____

Introduction to Category Problems

Homework

Write 4 things that belong in each box.

1. Foods

1. _____
2. _____
3. _____
4. _____

2. Animals

1. _____
2. _____
3. _____
4. _____

3. Colors

1. _____
2. _____
3. _____
4. _____

4. Clothes

1. _____
2. _____
3. _____
4. _____

5. Write a story problem about 2 things in one of the boxes. Solve it.

Student-Generated Category Problems **239**

Name _____

Remembering

Use sticks and circles to find change for a dollar.

1.

Soup 48¢

Change = [ ] ¢

2.

Pie 81¢

Change = [ ] ¢

Draw the time on each clock.

3.

| 11:30 |

4.

| 9:00 |

5.
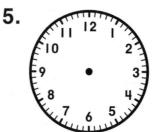
| 2:30 |

6.

| 5:00 |

Add the numbers.

7. $36 + 3 =$ [ ]

8. $46 + 6 =$ [ ]

9. $37 + 50 =$ [ ]

10. $79 + 5 =$ [ ]

11. $63 + 8 =$ [ ]

12. $49 + 30 =$ [ ]

Student-Generated Category Problems

Name _____

Homework

Solve the story problems.	**Show your work. Use pictures, numbers, or words.**
1. I saw 14 animals on my trip. 5 were moose, and the rest were deer. How many were deer? [ ] _____ label	 deer
2. Samantha has 26 apples and 15 bananas. How many pieces of fruit does she have? [ ] _____ label	 banana
3. There are 16 buildings downtown. 9 are stores, and the rest are banks. How many are banks? [ ] _____ label	 building
4. Our class made 54 shapes. 28 are triangles, and the rest are squares. How many are squares? [ ] _____ label	 shapes

Practice with Category Problems **241**

Name _____

Targeted Practice

Solve the story problems.

Show your work. Use pictures, numbers, or words.

---

1. On the shelf are 10 boxes of oatmeal and 9 boxes of puffed rice. How many cereal boxes are on the shelf?

cereal

☐ _____
　　　 label

---

2. There are 14 birds in the yard. 8 are sparrows, and the rest are robins. How many robins are there?

bird

☐ _____
　　　 label

---

3. Our patio has 25 roses and 32 daisies. How many flowers are on the patio?

flower

☐ _____
　　　 label

---

4. Our band has 16 instruments. 7 of them are drums, and the rest are horns. How many horns are there?

horn

☐ _____
　　　 label

Practice with Category Problems

Name _____

Homework

1. Ring the 10-partners. Find the total.

$7 + \boxed{(2 + 8)}^{10} = \square$ $3 + 7 + 9 = \square$ $6 + 5 + 5 = \square$

$4 + 6 + 5 = \square$ $9 + 1 + 6 = \square$ $8 + 7 + 2 = \square$

Solve the story problems.

Show your work. Use pictures, numbers, or words.

---

2. I drew 7 pictures of animals, 3 pictures of people, and 6 pictures of houses. How many pictures did I draw?

$\square$ _____
     label

picture

---

3. I have 9 white marbles, 5 blue marbles, and 3 green marbles. How many marbles do I have in all?

$\square$ _____
     label

marble

Remembering

Find the total price for each pair of things. Show your work.

1.  28¢   7¢   ☐ ¢

2. 56¢  9¢   ☐ ¢

3. 45¢   ✏ 8¢   ☐ ¢

4.	57	5.	63	6.	49	7.	38
	+ 26		+ 35		+ 19		+ 47

Solve the story problem.	Show your work. Use pictures, numbers, or words.
8. A worm ate 34 apples and 56 pears. How many pieces of fruit did the worm eat altogether? ☐ _____ label	 worm

Multiple-Step Addition Problems

Name _____

Homework

Solve these equations.

1. $7 + 3 - 8 =$ ☐ | **2.** $4 + 6 - 8 =$ ☐ | **3.** $8 + 5 - 3 =$ ☐

4. $4 + 5 - 5 =$ ☐ | **5.** $9 + 2 - 6 =$ ☐ | **6.** $3 + 6 - 9 =$ ☐

Solve the story problems.	**Show your work. Use pictures, numbers, or words.**

7. Raul borrowed 6 books from the library. He returned 3 of them and took out 2 more. How many books does he have now?

☐ _____
    label

book

8. Erica drew 10 shapes, but she erased 2 of them. Then she drew 6 more. How many shapes are there now?

☐ _____
    label

shapes

9. During our vacation there were 6 sunny days, 4 rainy days, and 5 cloudy days. How long was our vacation?

☐ _____
    label

rainy

Name _____

Remembering

Ring one half of the bears. Then fill in the blanks.

1.   One half of ___ is ___.

_____

2.   One half of ___ is ___.

_____

3.   One half of ___ is ___.

_____

Add the numbers.

4. 58 + 21	5. 44 + 37	6. 37 + 15	7. 29 + 48

_____

Count the money in each row.

8. ☐ ¢

_____

9. ☐ ¢

_____

10. ☐ ¢

Stories with Mixed Operations

Name _____

Homework

Solve these equations.

1. 70 + 20 + 8 = ☐

2. 50 + 30 − 20 = ☐

3. 40 + 30 + 6 = ☐

4. 60 + 20 − 10 = ☐

Solve the story problems.	Show your work. Use pictures, numbers, or words.

5. Reba planted 40 carrot seeds, 20 turnip seeds, and 7 melon seeds. How many seeds did she plant altogether?

☐ _____
label

turnip

6. In the woods we saw 20 wolf tracks, 30 deer tracks, and 6 bear tracks. How many animal tracks did we see?

☐ _____
label

wolf

7. The balloon man had 60 balloons. He sold 30. Then he lost 10 of them. How many balloons does he have now?

☐ _____
label

balloon

Multiple-Step Problems with Greater Numbers **247**

Remembering

How much change should you get back if you pay with a dollar?

1.

Folder 39¢

[ ] ¢

2.

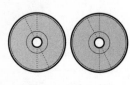

CDs 56¢

[ ] ¢

Add the numbers.

3. 47
    + 38

4. 82
    + 13

5. 53
    + 29

6. 26
    + 46

Solve the story problem.	**Show your work. Use pictures, numbers, or words.**

7. I have 5 hats, 9 shirts, and 2 jackets. How many pieces of clothing do I have?

jacket

[ ] _____
    label

Multiple-Step Problems with Greater Numbers

Name _____

Homework

Solve these equations.

1. $7 + 4 - 6 =$ ☐

2. $40 + 50 + 5 =$ ☐

3. $5 + 9 - 3 =$ ☐

4. $60 + 20 + 8 =$ ☐

Solve the story problems.	**Show your work. Use pictures, numbers, or words.**
5. Lisa stood at the flagpole. She took 12 steps forward and 4 steps back. Then she took 6 more steps forward. How far is Lisa from the flagpole? ☐ _____ label	 flagpole
6. Maria wants to jog 15 miles this week. By Wednesday she had jogged 9 miles. How many more miles does she need? ☐ _____ label	 jogger
7. At the fair, Jake rode the carousel 7 times yesterday and 6 times today. How many rides has he had? ☐ _____ label	 carousel

Name _____

Targeted Practice

Solve the story problems.

Show your work. Use pictures, numbers, or words.

---

1. My music book has 56 songs. Your book has 32 songs. How many songs do we have in all?

◻ _____
   label

music

---

2. I can carry 35 pounds in my backpack. My brother can carry 29 pounds. How many pounds can we carry together?

◻ _____
   label

backpack

---

3. A yogurt shop sold 48 cones yesterday and 37 cones today. How many cones were sold in all?

◻ _____
   label

cone

---

4. 12 teachers arrived on the bus. Then 13 more teachers came. How many are at school now?

◻ _____
   label

school

More Practice: Multiple-Step Problems

Name _____

Homework

Solve the story problems.	**Show your work. Use pictures, numbers, or words.**
1. Randy made 6 big snowmen, 6 little snowmen, and 2 snow forts. How many snowmen did he make? ⬜ _____ label	snowman
2. Tara got 5 birthday presents, 10 cards from friends, and 7 cards from her family. How many cards did she get? ⬜ _____ label	present
3. Enrico bought 9 blue balloons, 3 bags of popcorn, and 6 white ballons. How many balloons did he buy? ⬜ _____ label	popcorn
4. In the gym there are 4 helmets, 7 soccer balls, and 8 footballs. How many balls are there altogether? ⬜ _____ label	helmet

Remembering

Add the numbers by making a ten.

1. 5 + 2 + 8 = ☐ **2.** 3 + 7 + 8 = ☐ **3.** 9 + 5 + 5 = ☐

4. 6 + 4 + 3 = ☐ **5.** 1 + 9 + 6 = ☐ **6.** 8 + 4 + 2 = ☐

7. 2 + 8 + 7 = ☐ **8.** 4 + 5 + 6 = ☐ **9.** 6 + 3 + 7 = ☐

Solve the story problem.

Show your work. Use pictures, numbers, or words.

10. Mira's garden has 8 daisies, 5 roses, and 2 scarecrows. How many flowers does Mira have?

scarecrow

☐ _____
        label

Add the numbers.

11. 37
      + 42

12. 73
      + 17

13. 52
      + 29

14. 49
      + 46

Find Essential Information

Name _____

Homework

Solve the story problems.	Show your work. Use pictures, numbers, or words.

1. Manuela bought 8 red pencils, 8 blue pencils, and 3 books. How many pencils did she buy in all?

⬜ _____
label

pencil

---

2. Simon has 7 striped caps, 6 green socks, and 8 blue caps. What is the total number of caps?

⬜ _____
label

sock

---

3. My family has 7 pairs of skis, 5 pairs of ice skates, and 6 pairs of roller skates. How many pairs of skates do we have?

⬜ _____
label

ice skate

---

4. On our trip we saw 38 deer, 6 lakes, and 25 moose. How many animals did we see altogether?

⬜ _____
label

moose

Name _____

Targeted Practice

Solve the story problems.

Show your work. Use pictures, numbers, or words.

1. On the swings are 8 boys, 5 girls, and 2 spiders. How many children are on the swings?

[ ] _____
      label

spider

2. Mr. Reuben made 6 cheese sandwiches, 7 tuna sandwiches, and 12 cookies. How many sandwiches did he make?

[ ] _____
      label

sandwich

3. A carpenter has 8 hammers, 6 saws, and 3 hats. How many tools does he have?

[ ] _____
      label

carpenter

4. There are 10 houses, 3 stores, and 6 trees on Pine Road. How many buildings are there?

[ ] _____
      label

house

Practice with Extra Information

Homework

Name _____

Solve the story problems.	Show your work. Use pictures, numbers, or words.

1. A kangaroo went 12 hops forward, 8 hops backward, and 5 hops forward again. How far is he from where he started?

[ ] _____
label

kangaroo

2. Ramon put 8 knives, 16 forks, and 8 spoons on the table. How many things are on the table?

[ ] _____
label

knife

3. My father bought 42 oranges, 35 lemons, and 6 shirts. How many pieces of fruit did he buy?

[ ] _____
label

lemon

4. On the Back Write a story problem with extra numbers. Then solve it.

Consolidation: Story Problem Festival

Homework

Cut out the strips on the bottom of the page.
Use them to measure the trains.
Round up or down.

1.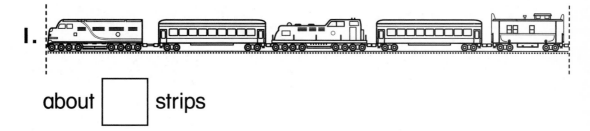

about ⬚ strips

2.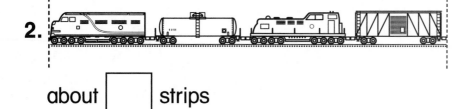

about ⬚ strips

3.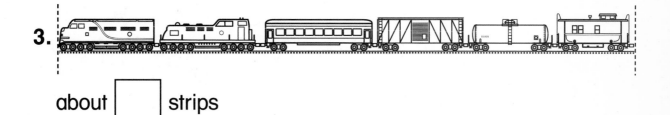

about ⬚ strips

4.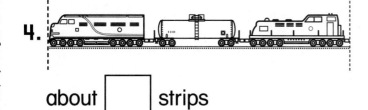

about ⬚ strips

5.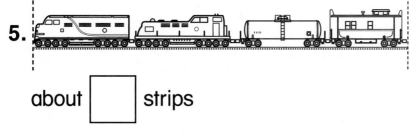

about ⬚ strips

✂

Measurement: Nonstandard Units and Rounding

Name _____

Targeted Practice

Solve the story problems.	Show your work. Use pictures, numbers, or words.

---

1. Today we saw 30 sailboats, 20 rowboats, and 10 trains. How many boats did we see?

sailboat

```
┌──────┐
│      │  _____
└──────┘
      label
```

---

2. Mia has 28 white seashells, 26 grey rocks, and 25 pink seashells. How many seashells does Mia have?

seashell

```
┌──────┐
│      │  _____
└──────┘
      label
```

---

3. On the farm, I saw 6 horses, 4 tractors, and 8 cows. How many farm animals did I see?

tractor

```
┌──────┐
│      │  _____
└──────┘
      label
```

➜ **On the Back** Write an addition story problem about 4 apples, 7 bananas, and 6 oranges. Add extra information about some pencils. Then solve to find how many pieces of fruit in all.

Measurement: Nonstandard Units and Rounding **259**

Measurement: Nonstandard and Rounding

Homework

Cut out the ruler or use your own ruler.

Measure some things at home.

Write the name of each thing. About how long is it?

1. I measured _____.

   It is about _____ inches long.

2. I measured _____.

   It is about _____ inches long.

3. I measured _____.

   It is about _____ inches long.

4. I measured _____.

   It is about _____ inches long.

5. I measured _____.

   It is about _____ inches long.

9
8
7
6
5
4
3
2
1
0 inches

Name _____

Remembering

Use sticks and circles to find change for a dollar.

1.
Marker 59¢

Change = ☐ ¢

2.
Notebook 76¢

Change = ☐ ¢

Measure each string in inches.

3.

☐ inches

☐ inches

☐ inches

☐ inches

Continue the pattern.

4. 5 10 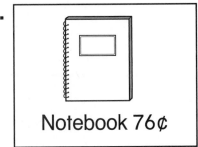 15 ⚫

⬤ **On the Back** Suppose a pencil costs 22¢. How much change would you get back if you paid with a quarter?

Exploration with Inches **263**

Exploration with Inches

Name _____

Homework

Measure each piece of string to the nearest inch.

1. 〰〰〰〰〰〰〰〰〰 about [ ] in.

2. 〰〰〰〰〰〰〰〰〰〰〰〰〰 about [ ] in.

3. 〰〰〰〰 about [ ] in.

4.

5.

6.

about [ ] in.

about [ ] in.

about [ ] in.

about [ ] in.

9
8
7
6
5
4
3
2
1
0

inches

Use an Inch Ruler **265**

Name

Targeted Practice

Measure each piece of string to the nearest inch.

1. ~~~~~~~~~~~~~~~~ about ☐ in.

2. ~~~~~~~~~~~~~~~~~~ about ☐ in.

3. ~~~~~~~ about ☐ in.

4.

5.

6.

about ☐ in.

about ☐ in.

about ☐ in.

9
8
7
6
5
4
3
2
1
0 inches

Use an Inch Ruler **267**

Name _____

Homework

Measure the sides of each gray shape with an inch ruler.

1.

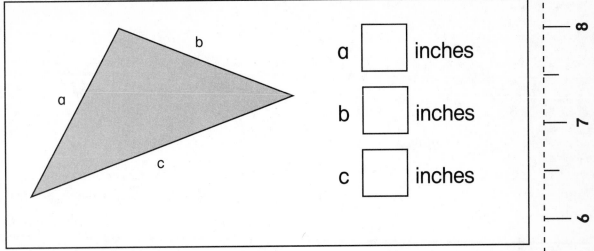

a [ ] inches

b [ ] inches

c [ ] inches

2.

a [ ]
inch

b [ ]
inch

c [ ]
inch

d [ ]
inch

Square? _____

3.

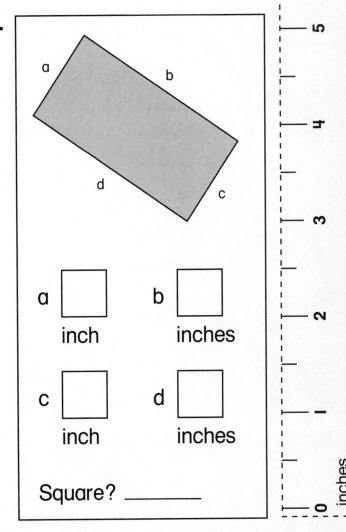

a [ ]
inch

b [ ]
inches

c [ ]
inch

d [ ]
inches

Square? _____

Measure Shapes in Inches **269**

9
8
7
6
5
4
3
2
1
0

inches

Name _____

Targeted Practice

Measure each ribbon to the nearest inch.

1. ///////////////////////////// about [ ] inches

2. ▓▓▓▓▓▓▓▓▓ about [ ] inches

3. <<<<<<<<<<<<<<<<<<< about [ ] inches

4. •••••••••••••• about [ ] inches

Estimate how many inches.
Then measure and write the length.

5. ▨▨▨▨▨▨▨▨▨

   Estimate: about [ ] inches   Measure: [ ] inches

6. ◇◇◇◇◇◇◇◇

   Estimate: about [ ] inches   Measure: [ ] inches

7. ///////////////////////////

   Estimate: about [ ] inches   Measure: [ ] inches

🔵 **On the Back** Use words or pictures to explain the rule for rounding.

Measure Shapes in Inches

Homework

Cut out the rulers. Measure the chains in centimeters. Then measure them in inches. Round the numbers. Fill in the table.

Chain	Centimeters	Inches
A	_____ cm	about _____ in.
B	_____ cm	about _____ in.
C	_____ cm	about _____ in.
D	_____ cm	about _____ in.

A

B

C

D

20 19 18 17 16 15 14 13 12 11 10 9 8 7 6 5 4 3 2 1 0
centimeters

9 8 7 6 5 4 3 2 1 0
inches

Name _____

Remembering

Measure the strings in inches. Round to the nearest inch.

1. ∿∿∿∿∿∿∿∿∿∿∿∿∿∿∿∿ about ☐ inches

2. ∿∿∿∿∿∿∿∿ about ☐ inches

3. ∿∿∿∿∿∿∿∿∿∿∿ about ☐ inches

4. ∿∿∿∿∿∿∿∿∿∿∿∿∿∿∿∿∿ about ☐ inches

Draw the time on each clock.

5.

6.

7.

8.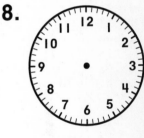

| 12 : 30 | 7 : 00 | 3 : 30 | 4 : 00 |

Add the numbers.

9. 45 + 3 = ☐   **10.** 56 + 7 = ☐   **11.** 39 + 50 = ☐

12. 78 + 4 = ☐   **13.** 83 + 8 = ☐   **14.** 46 + 30 = ☐

On the Back Use a ruler to draw a rectangle that is 2 inches wide and 4 inches long.

Use a Centimeter Ruler

Homework

Cut out the rulers. Measure some things at home. Round the numbers. Fill in the table below.

Object	Centimeters	Inches
Spoon		
Fork		
Toothbrush		

centimeters

inches

Measure Shapes in Centimeters

Name _____

Remembering

Measure the length and width of each rectangle in centimeters.

1.

[rectangle]

[ ] cm   [ ] cm
length   width

2.

[ ] cm   [ ] cm
length   width

Add the numbers.

3.   58
       + 39

4.   74
       + 12

5.   43
       + 29

6.   27
       + 37

Solve the problem.	**Show your work. Use pictures, numbers, or words.**

7. A quilt has 24 green pieces and 36 white pieces. How many pieces are there in all?

[ ] _____
          label

quilt

⬢ **On the Back** Draw a rectangle with a length of 4 cm and a width of 2 cm.

Measure Shapes in Centimeters **279**

Measure Shapes in Centimeters

Homework

How far did each bug jump?
Measure in centimeters and inches.
Round the numbers. Fill in the table.

A |————————————————|

B |————————————————————————————|

C |——————————————————————————————————|

D |——————————————————————————————|

Bug	Centimeters	Inches
A	about _____ cm	about _____ in.
B	about _____ cm	about _____ in.
C	about _____ cm	about _____ in.
D	about _____ cm	about _____ in.

Comparative Measurements: Centimeters and Inches **281**

centimeters

inches

Comparative Measurements: Centimeters and Inches

Name _____

Remembering

A B C D

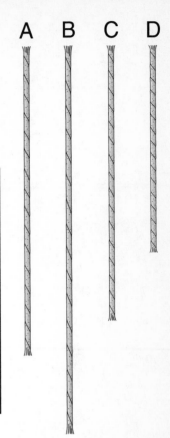

Measure the pieces of yarn in centimeters.

Then measure them in inches.

Round the numbers. Fill in the table.

I.

Yarn	Centimeters	Inches
A	about _____ cm	about _____ in.
B	about _____ cm	about _____ in.
C	about _____ cm	about _____ in.
D	about _____ cm	about _____ in.

Solve the story problem.

Show your work. Use pictures, numbers, or words.

2. There were 15 fish.

Then 7 swam away.

How many fish are left?

[ ] _____
      label

fish

Add the numbers.

3. 66
    + 23

4. 27
    + 19

5. 28
    + 43

6. 35
    + 39

 On the Back Write a story problem using centimeters.

Comparative Measurements: Centimeters and Inches